STRANGE NATURE

Written by
Joyce Pope

Illustrated by
Adam Hook and Helen Ward

RSVP
**RAINTREE
STECK-VAUGHN**
PUBLISHERS
The Steck-Vaughn Company

Austin, Texas

Editors: Andy Charman and Wendy Madgwick
Designer: Mike Jolley
Picture research: Jenny Faithfull
Front cover: chameleon
Back cover: praying mantis

Library of Congress Cataloging-in-Publication Data

Pope, Joyce.
Strange nature / written by Joyce Pope;
illustrated by Adam Hook and Helen Ward.
p. cm. – (Curious creatures)
Includes index.
Summary: Examines some of the wonders of nature, under such
headings as "Strange Habitats," "Strange Families," and "Staying Alive."
ISBN 0-8114-6259-5 (softcover)
1. Zoology – Miscellanea – Juvenile literature.
[1. Nature – Miscellanea. 2. Animals – Miscellanea.]
I. Hook, Adam, ill. II. Ward, Helen, 1962- ill. III. Title. IV. Series.
QL49.P748   1992   91-46092
591.5–dc20   CIP AC

NOTES TO READER

There are some words in this book which are printed in **bold** type.
A brief explanation of these words is given in the glossary on p. 45.

All living things are given a Latin name when first classified by a scientist.
Some of them also have a common name. For example, the common name
of *Sturnus vulgaris* is common starling. In this book we use other Latin words,
such as larva and pupa. We make these words plural by adding an "e,"
for example, one larva becomes many larvae (pronounced lar-vee).

Color separations by Positive Colour Ltd., Maldon, Essex, Great Britain
Printed and bound by L.E.G.O., Vicenza, Italy
1 2 3 4 5 6 7 8 9 0 LE 96 95 94 93 92

CONTENTS

THE LIVING PLANET

The planet Earth may be the only place in the universe where life as we know it exists. Some scientists think that there could be others. Even so, as yet, none has been found, although galaxies beyond our own have been searched. Perhaps we should say that life itself is strange.

Earth has the right combination of minerals, atmosphere, and temperature for living things to thrive. Plants grow almost everywhere there is light. Some even grow on ice sheets. Others survive in springs near volcanoes, where the temperature of the water is close to boiling. Almost everywhere that plants are found, animals are present to feed on them.

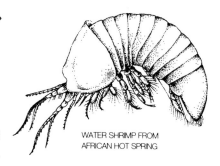

WATER SHRIMP FROM
AFRICAN HOT SPRING

▲▼ The boiling water bubbles from the ground in hot springs like this one in Yellowstone National Park. You would be badly scalded if you were to try to swim there. Yet a few kinds of small plants and tiny animals are able to spend all of their lives in such places.

TRICHAPTUS FROM BRAZIL

VIOLIN BEETLE
FROM JAVA

CLYTOSTYLUS FROM PHILIPPINES

▲ The trees of tropical forests, like
this one in Brazil, do not all shed
their leaves at the same time. There
are always some with flowers and
fruit. As a result, there is never any
shortage of food. This environment is
home for more kinds of creatures
than anywhere else on Earth. The
treetops make a living place for
brilliant birds and insects, as well
as mammals such as monkeys
and bats.

Scientists have so far discovered and described over
a million different kinds of animals. Many more remain
to be found. Some people say that the total, when we
know them all, will be at least 8 million.

Most life is found in moist, warm parts of the world.
In such places, different kinds of animals crowd together
to use the **environment** as fully as possible. In spite of
this, no two species that live in the same place have
exactly the same way of life. Some have developed very
strange techniques in order to survive at all. This book is
about some of these extraordinary animals.

STRANGE HABITATS

▼ Very little rain falls in the central part of Australia. In spite of this, many creatures live there. Emus usually prefer places with more plants, though they sometimes produce their young in very dry areas. Many **reptiles** survive in extreme deserts. So do a few mammals such as the kowaris, which are tiny, insect-eating relatives of the kangaroos. They can go without drinking for their entire lifetime.

Most animals can survive only where there is warmth and moisture. Some creatures, however, make their homes in deserts or icy seas. Their bodies have become adapted to these hostile environments.

DESERT ANIMALS

Deserts may be hot, like the Sahara in Africa, or they may be cold, like Antarctica, but they are all places where there is less than 5 inches of rain in a year.

EMUS

SKINK

GOULD'S GOANNA

◀ Musk oxen are the largest animals able to survive on land in the Arctic. Beneath their long, shaggy coats is an underfur so fine and dense that it keeps them warm in the coldest weather. They do not **migrate** to warmer places in the winter, but stay to feed on the tough **tundra** plants.

Incredible Insects

One of the strangest living places in the world is the pools of crude oil that seep to the top of the ground in some parts of America. These are the home of a small fly called *Halaeomysis*. The adults can walk over the oil and are unaffected by the poisonous fumes. Only their feet are protected. If another part of their body touches the oil, they become stuck. Their **larvae** hatch from eggs laid close to the oil pools. The larvae move into the oil and swim through it with only the tips of their breathing tubes showing above the surface. They eat any small trapped creature – sometimes even their own parents.

HALAEOMYSIS

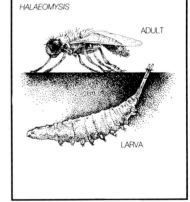

ADULT

LARVA

Because there is so little water, few plants can grow. Most desert animals are small. In hot deserts, the largest is the camel.

We see camels in zoos and in films, and so we forget what strange creatures they are. A camel does not feel heat as much as most other animals do. Its thick coat acts as a blanket to **insulate** it. Like other creatures, a camel's body is made largely of water. It must have water to drink, but it can go without liquid far longer than most other large animals. It can lose up to one-third of its body weight from thirst, and then drink up to 7 gallons in ten minutes to make it up!

MOLOCH (THORNY DEVIL)

INLAND TAIPAN

KOWARIS (DESERT MICE)

IN FROZEN SEAS

There are two reasons why most animals cannot survive in very cold places. One is that there is very little food. Plants need warmth for growth and even flesh eaters depend on animals that have eaten plants. The other reason is that animals die if they freeze. This is because their cells break apart if ice crystals form in their bodies.

Mammals such as polar bears and birds such as penguins are sometimes found in very cold places. They are **warm-blooded** and use a lot of energy to heat their bodies so that they do not freeze. Also, they have thick coats of fur or feathers and a layer of fat beneath their skin to help keep them warm.

Cold-blooded animals, such as snakes, frogs, and fishes, get warmth from their surroundings. As a result, we do not find them in icy places. Yet some fishes can survive in the Antarctic Ocean. They are found in places so cold that the surface of the water is covered with ice for ten months of the year. Beneath this, the temperature of the sea is permanently below 32°F. The fish do not become frozen solid because their cells contain special chemicals that act as an antifreeze.

▶ The "antifreeze" fish of the Antarctic are mostly slow-moving creatures, which often swim using their large pectoral (shoulder) fins. Most live near the seafloor, well away from ice crystals, which are mainly in the upper waters. Contact with the ice could cause the fish's supercooled blood to freeze.

▼ Crabeater seals, like these, live mainly on Antarctic pack ice. Breathing holes, such as the one shown here, are made by Weddell seals, but they are often used by the crabeaters. In spite of their name, crabeaters feed almost entirely on shrimplike creatures called krill, which the seals sieve from the water with their pointed teeth.

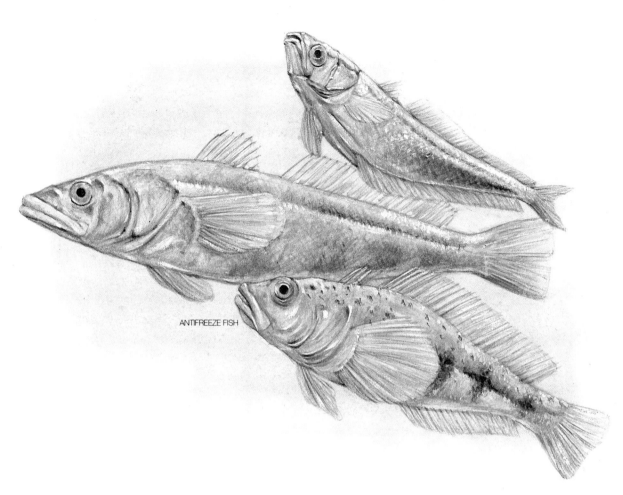

ANTIFREEZE FISH

Volcanic Vent Animals

There are some hot spots in the cold depths of the oceans, where volcanic eruptions occur on the seabed. Nothing can live where lava flows, but in some places near-boiling water spouts out through cracks or vents. This water contains many chemicals. These provide the basic needs of microscopic organisms called **bacteria**. The bacteria are the food for giant worms, crabs, and clams. These animals are different from all other creatures in the world. Their energy comes not from the sun but from underwater volcanoes. They live entirely without light or contact with any other living things.

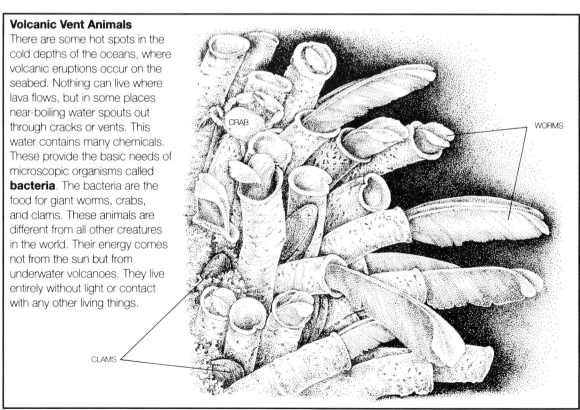

CRAB

WORMS

CLAMS

GRASSHOPPER

BEETLE

BUTTERFLY

FLIGHTLESS INSECTS

▲ Insects that are carried by freak winds to oceanic islands often change greatly in the course of time. Many, like those shown here, lose their power of flight. Also they often increase in size, for there is usually plenty of food for growth.

ISLAND ANIMALS

Some islands, like Great Britain and Japan, have been cut off from nearby continents by changes in sea level. Great Britain, for instance, was finally cut off from the rest of Europe about 4,000 years ago. Islands like these are called continental islands. The plants and animals found there are the same as those on the nearby mainlands. Some, called oceanic islands, are the tips of volcanoes rising from the deep sea. These islands have no connection with any other land, and the creatures that live there are almost always quite different from any others.

The reason for this is that animals reach these distant islands by accident. Small birds or insects may be blown by freak winds. Small mammals and reptiles may arrive by sea on mats of vegetation. Most of these creatures die, but if they land on a new island, provided that plants have arrived before them, they find themselves in a world where they have no enemies and no competitors for food. Survival is easy, especially for small animals. In time they may change so that they can eat a wider variety of food.

The descendants of winged creatures often become flightless. Most islands are windy places, so flying can mean being blown away. As a result, groups of volcanic islands, such as the Galapagos and Hawaii, have some of the strangest animals in the world.

FLIGHTLESS BIRDS

KIWI

CASSOWARY

DODO

▲ Komodo dragons, shown here, come only from the small island of Komodo in Indonesia. In spite of their name, they are lizards, related to the monitors of other parts of the tropics. But like many reptiles from remote islands, they have become giant-sized, sometimes growing to a length of over 10 feet. They are the largest lizards in the world.

◄ Most kinds of island birds are dull-colored because there is less competition for living space than on mainlands and so the birds do not need to display to defend their territories. On a windy island, flying can be dangerous, so many birds have become flightless. They also tend to grow in size. Their large size and being flightless is fine so long as they have no competitors. But if their island is invaded by humans, who may bring predators, they may die out, like the dodo.

The Same, but Different

The upland forests of the islands of Hawaii are the home of some strange birds called Hawaiian honeycreepers. There are 14 living species, which are all very similar in many ways. Most are brightly colored and males and females usually look alike. So far as is known, their courtship, nests, and eggs are also alike. Only their beaks are very different because some feed on insects, some on seeds, and some on nectar.

Scientists think that several million years ago a small flock of birds got blown to Hawaii by an unusual wind. Over the centuries since then, their descendants have taken to feeding on a variety of foods. Their beaks have changed with their feeding habits. Yet basically, these birds are still very similar.

HAWAIIAN HONEYCREEPERS

FRUIT AND SEED EATER

NECTAR FEEDER

INSECT AND NECTAR FEEDER

INSECT GRUB EATER

INSECT EATER

WALKING ON WATER

If you look at a pond you will see that there are many creatures swimming in the water. Others, such as springtails and pond skaters, seem to be walking on the water surface. This is possible because the surface of the water is slightly different from the water below. It behaves as if it were covered with a thin, stretchy sheet of plastic. Anything heavy goes right through, but lightweight creatures merely dent it. Anything that lives in this way has the advantage of being able to escape from land-based enemies. It is also safe from most **predators** in the water below.

The water is not kind to all small creatures. If they fall in, they may be trapped by the surface film. Pond skaters have special hairs on their legs that are sensitive to movements in the water. They will rush to attack and eat any small creature caught by the surface film. Pond skaters have a rival in the fisher spiders. These spiders

▼ Insects and spiders such as those shown below have oily hairs on their feet. Although they may dent the surface film of the water, the tiny quantity of oil keeps them from sinking as they rush to catch creatures that are not so well protected and have become trapped in the water.

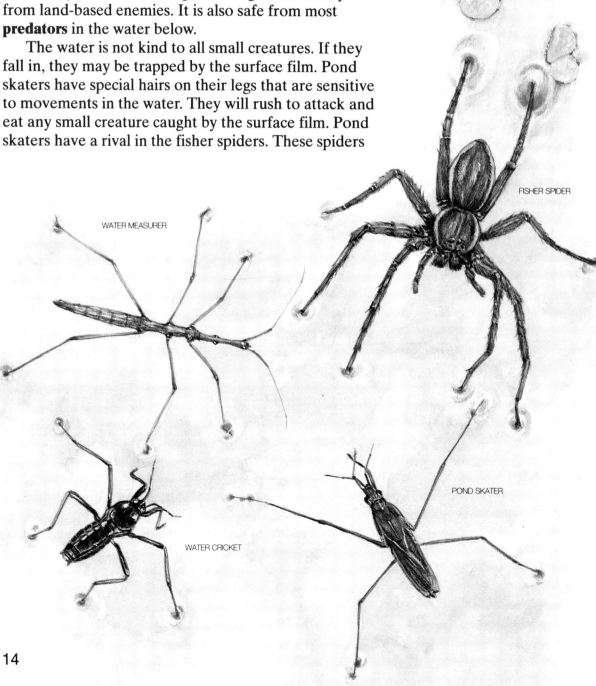

FISHER SPIDER

WATER MEASURER

WATER CRICKET

POND SKATER

14

normally sit by the edge of the water, with two legs resting on the surface to feel for ripples made by small creatures. When they detect such movements, the spiders dash across the water to grab their meal. They sometimes even catch tiny fishes and tadpoles that have come too close to the surface.

▲ Basilisk lizards spend most of their life in trees, but when on land they can run at nearly 6 miles an hour. At this speed, the basilisk can escape from its enemies by running across water supported by the surface film. But it is too heavy to be carried for long and sinks after a few paces.

Lily Trotters and Wave Hoppers

Birds called lily trotters walk over the water of tropical lakes. They are supported by the large, flat leaves of water lilies. The birds' long toes spread their weight, but they sink through the surface film if they slip off the leaves.

In some of the stormiest seas of the world, flocks of little, dark-colored birds flutter over the slopes of the waves, picking up tiny scraps of food. They look as if they are running over the water. These birds are called petrels and are named after St. Peter, who is said to have walked on the water. Petrels half-run and half-fly, but they do not dive and swim underwater, as do most other birds of the open oceans.

PETREL

LILY TROTTER

STRANGE PARTNERS

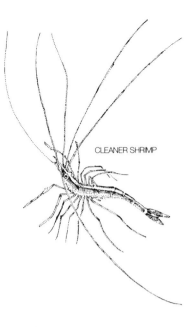

CLEANER SHRIMP

Most animals take very little notice of the other kinds of creatures that live around them. Animals that are hunted recognize predators and avoid them if possible. Apart from this, even though an animal may share the same environment, including its food and water, with others, each species has its own way of life.

NEEDING ONE ANOTHER

There are exceptions to this general rule. They usually occur when one species provides food for another in such a way that both parties benefit. For instance, you

▲▼ Barber, or cleaner, fish like the one in the photograph and cleaner shrimps are two kinds of creatures that are often found with fishes big enough to eat them. But they are not attacked because they feed on parasites that live on the fishes. On coral reefs, fishes often swim to places where large numbers of cleaners live. The cleaners get an easy meal, and the fishes lose their annoying parasites.

can sometimes see a bird sitting on the back of a large mammal. The bird is not just hitching a ride, but feeding on **parasites** that live on the mammal. The bird and the mammal can manage quite well without each other, but they do better together. The bird benefits because it gets an easy meal, the mammal because it loses its parasites.

Some kinds of animals are almost always associated with members of another species. For instance, some big tropical sea anemones often have damselfish living in and around them. In some cases, the partnership becomes so close that neither can survive without the other. This is so with some kinds of termites. They have single-celled animals living in their guts. These help the termites to digest food. If they die, so do the termites.

HONEY GUIDE

RATEL

▲ In Africa, small birds called honey guides attract the attention of mammals, particularly the honey badger, or ratel. The ratel follows the bird to a bee's nest, which it breaks open to feed on the honey and grubs. When the ratel has finished, the bird flies down to feed on the remains.

A Living Home

Many hermit crabs carry sea anemones on their shells. This is no accident – the crabs put them there. The main reason is that the anemones' stinging tentacles protect the crabs against octopuses, which are their chief enemies. In return, the anemones get food, for hermit crabs are untidy eaters, often dropping morsels of food. A cloak anemone, which is sometimes seen on a hermit crab's shell, lies with its mouth below the crab's head to catch scraps of food. Besides protecting the crab, the anemone provides it with a home. As the crab grows, so does the base of the anemone. This, in the end, enlarges the shell in which the crab lives. With a cloak anemone, the crab never needs to look for another shell.

CALLIACTIS ANEMONE

HERMIT CRABS WITH SEA ANEMONES ON THEIR SHELLS

CLOAK ANEMONE

LODGING WITH ANTS

There may be more than half a million ants in a single **colony**. Most species of ants have large jaws, stingers, and acid with which to defend themselves. Only large or well-protected animals dare to attack them. Yet most ants' nests contain a large number of roomers.

Many kinds of beetles are found in ants' nests. Some of them earn their way by helping to keep the nest clean. Other beetles are parasites, feeding on the ants' **grubs**. They escape detection because they look, and probably smell, like the ants.

Some inhabitants of ants' nests pay for their keep in a different way. They produce a sweet substance called honeydew. The ants eat this and are prepared to feed these guests to get the honeydew. Caterpillars of the large blue butterfly spend most of their lives in the nests of certain kinds of ants. The eggs hatch in the open, and the caterpillars feed on plants. Eventually, ants find them and carry them to their nests. The caterpillars give the ants honeydew and are fed on the ants' grubs. When the caterpillars turn into **chrysalises**, the ants do not harm them. Newly hatched butterflies must find their way out of the ants' nest before their wings stretch and harden. This hardening takes much longer than in most other butterflies, so they reach the open without damage.

ANTS CARRYING
A CATERPILLAR
TO THEIR NEST

▼ ▲ When the ants find a caterpillar of the large blue butterfly, they carry it back to their nest. It is fed on grubs and produces honeydew, on which the ants feed. After hatching from its chrysalis, the butterfly makes its way to the surface.

LARGE BLUE BUTTERFLY MAKING
ITS WAY TO THE SURFACE

◀ The large blue butterfly shown here is not the only species of butterfly to associate with ants. Ants feed on the honeydew produced by caterpillars of some other kinds of blue butterflies, such as the chalk hill blue in Europe and the silvery blue in North America, but do not protect them in their nests.

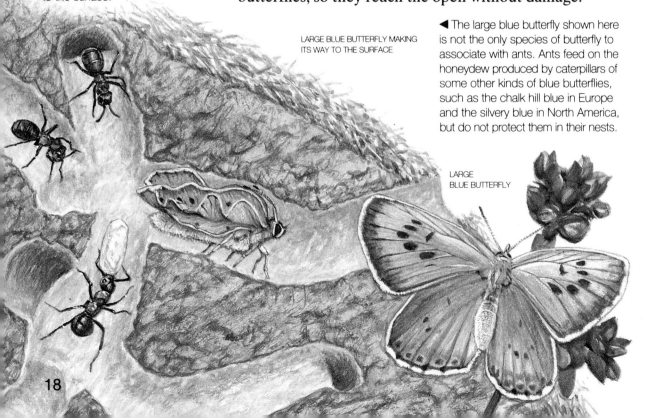

LARGE
BLUE BUTTERFLY

Farmer Ants

Some insects, such as aphids (greenflies) feed on the sweet sap of plants. This contains more sugar than they need, so they turn some of it into honeydew. Ants tap the aphids with their antennae (see photo below) to encourage them to produce drops of honeydew. They often protect colonies of aphids, driving away or killing other creatures that might harm them. Some kinds of ants even take the eggs of aphids back to their nests and care for them through the winter. When spring comes, they carry the eggs out to suitable plants for the aphids to feed on. In this way, the ants are sure to have a supply of honeydew through the summer.

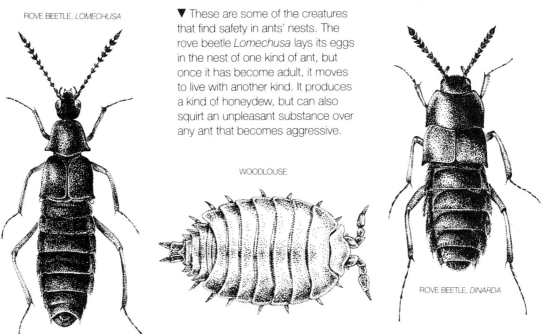

ROVE BEETLE, *LOMECHUSA*

▼ These are some of the creatures that find safety in ants' nests. The rove beetle *Lomechusa* lays its eggs in the nest of one kind of ant, but once it has become adult, it moves to live with another kind. It produces a kind of honeydew, but can also squirt an unpleasant substance over any ant that becomes aggressive.

WOODLOUSE

ROVE BEETLE, *DINARDA*

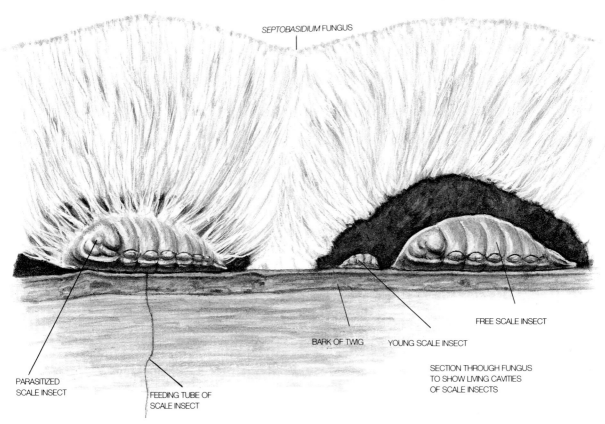

SEPTOBASIDIUM FUNGUS

PARASITIZED
SCALE INSECT

FEEDING TUBE OF
SCALE INSECT

BARK OF TWIG

YOUNG SCALE INSECT

FREE SCALE INSECT

SECTION THROUGH FUNGUS
TO SHOW LIVING CAVITIES
OF SCALE INSECTS

ANIMALS AND PLANTS

All plants and animals depend on each other. Plants make food for animals, and animals help the plants in many ways. Some trees use ants for protection. As the ants search for food, they run over the twigs and leaves. Scientists have discovered that if they remove the ants, the tree is attacked and damaged by animals that feed on its leaves and branches.

The strangest partnership between plants and animals is one that most people would not notice. It involves a kind of **fungus** and **scale insects** that live here in North America. The fungus covers the branches of many kinds of trees with a whitish blanket. Scale insects live under the fungus and suck juices from the tree. They never need to move away because they are well protected. Some of the insects cannot move because the fungus sends down threads into their bodies, and feeds on them. But the insects are not killed by this. In fact they live longer than those not invaded by the fungus. The free scale insects are able to produce young, some of which will eventually be attacked by the fungus. The fungus uses the insects as a means of acquiring food – some insects are eaten and others produce young for future use. You could say that the plant had domesticated the animals.

▲ This picture shows the unusual fungus called *Septobasidium*. Beneath its wrinkled surface, which is all that can be seen on a branch, are the "stables" in which scale insects are kept. When they are very young, some of the scale insects move out onto the tree branch, but few survive, for they are attacked by parasites or predators.

▶ Whistling thorns are spiny acacia trees that live in dry parts of Africa. As each spine grows, the base swells and is soft for a short time. Tiny ants gnaw out the tender inner part of the thorn, and then, as it hardens, make their nests in the pot-shaped holes. They defend the trees by running out and attacking any browsing animals. The small entrance holes to the ants' nests are like the holes in a flute. As the wind blows across them, they make an eerie whistling sound.

Animal Gardeners

Some beetles from New Guinea are known as gardeners because plants grow on their backs. These plants serve as **camouflage**. Their furrowed wing cases provide plenty of room for plants, such as **lichens** and **mosses**. These are miniature forests with tiny animals living in them. Some of these animals have only been found on the backs of these weevils.

Other gardeners live in the sea. They are spider crabs, sometimes known as decorator crabs. They disguise themselves by attaching bits of seaweed or sponge to hooked hairs on their shells and legs. Some of the seaweed continues to grow on the crab – often more successfully than it did before.

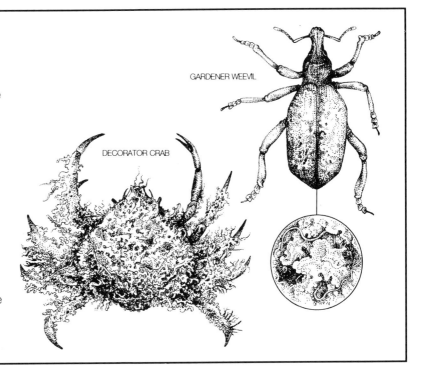

GARDENER WEEVIL

DECORATOR CRAB

STRANGE FAMILIES

We usually think of a family as parents and their children of different ages, but this is not the case for most animals. Almost all young creatures are left to take their chances in the world, so they never know their mothers and fathers. Yet many other animals are always part of single-parent families.

MOTHERS ALONE

The strangest one-parent families are the vast colonies of ants, bees, and wasps. Each colony has the same mother, known as the queen. Apart from a few males, most members of a colony are called workers. They are all females, though they are unable to produce young of their own.

▶ The workers in a colony of naked mole rats may make more than 980 feet of tunnels that radiate from the central living chambers. The babies shown here will become workers when they are about 3 months old, though they will not be fully grown until they are a year old.

▼ Aphids, or greenflies, like the ones shown below, do not have to mate with a male to produce young. Their young are born fully formed, rather than as eggs. In summer the young aphids are all females, and can soon give birth themselves. In autumn, some males are born. These mate with the females, which then lay eggs that can survive the winter. Next spring, the eggs hatch into females.

One kind of mammal lives in a society like that of the **social insects**. This is the naked mole rat, which comes from very dry parts of East Africa. As many as 30 animals all live together. Their mother is the leader of the group. She is much larger than all the rest. With her are several slightly smaller non-workers. The rest of the family are all workers. They dig the tunnels and find food for the whole group. They are all very much smaller than the non-workers, even when they are adult. Only the mother produces young. When she dies, one of the female non-workers is likely to take her place.

NAKED MOLE RATS

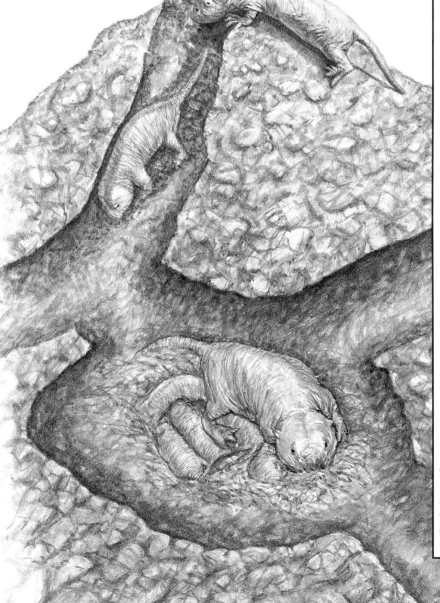

Water Fleas

In spite of their name, water fleas are more closely related to crabs than to real fleas. One strange thing about them is that, most of the time, all water fleas are females. They produce young without mating with males. The young are always females and, soon after they are born, they have families of their own. Only when conditions become unsuitable for active survival are some males born. After mating with them, the females lay eggs. These eggs are surrounded by very tough cases and can remain alive even in very cold weather. If the water dries up, the eggs may be blown about. They will hatch into females once they arrive in a pond or stream again.

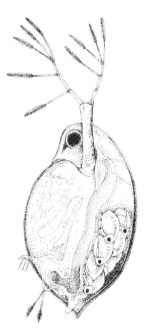

WATER FLEA WITH YOUNG
ABOUT TO BE BORN

On land, aphids have a similar way of life. It is a good method of survival for small creatures that are food for many other animals. Only one individual needs to escape for the population to build up again.

FATHERS' FAMILIES

Some male animals help to look after their families. A dog fox, for instance, brings food to the **vixen** and newborn cubs. When they are older, he helps to catch food for them and to guard them. Some creatures go further than this. Some male frogs and toads care for their eggs and tadpoles. Darwin's frog swallows the eggs soon after they are laid, keeping them safe in his throat pouch. They do not leave until they have changed into frogs.

Many male fishes care for their young. Some, like sticklebacks, guard the nest, watching over the young fishes, or fry. Some carry the eggs in their mouths. Pipefish and sea horses go even further. The female lays the eggs into a pouch on the underside of the male's body. Safe inside the pouch, the **embryos** in the eggs get oxygen and food from their father. Finally, the male fish gives birth. This is easy for pipefish, for the pouch has a long, slit-like opening. The little fish can even return to safety if danger threatens. Male sea horses keep their young for longer. They are larger and cannot return to the pouch as the pipefish do.

▶ The pouch of a male pipefish, shown here, is a long slit on its underside. As soon as they are born, the little fish rush to the surface of the water to take a bubble of air. This enables their swim bladders to work. After this, they only return to the safety of their father's pouch if danger threatens.

▼ The pictures below show some frogs and fishes in which the males care for their families. In most cases, the caring male frogs live in very warm climates. Sticklebacks and most kinds of sea horses live in cooler places.

MALE DARWIN'S FROG

MALE SEA HORSE GIVING BIRTH

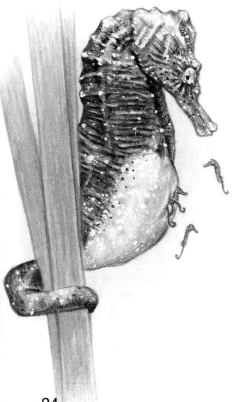

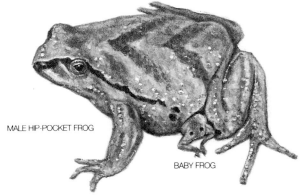

MALE HIP-POCKET FROG

BABY FROG

MALE STICKLEBACK GUARDING NEST

MALE POISON ARROW FROG
CARRYING TADPOLES

Rhea Fathers

Rheas are ostrichlike birds that live in South America. Males fight in the breeding season to drive away rivals. The victor then displays to several females, finally leading them to a nest that he has made. Over several days, as many as six females may lay their eggs there. In the end the male often has a clutch of 30 eggs to look after. The females leave without taking care of the eggs at all. The male incubates them alone for about seven weeks. The fluffy chicks are able to run around soon after they hatch. Their father watches over them and leads them around to find food.

MALE RHEA AND CHICKS

NURSERY LIFE

A few creatures make special cradles for their eggs or young. One of the curious things that people sometimes find by the sea is a "sand collar." This contains the eggs of a moon shell, keeping them safe from fishes and most enemies. At sea, the paper nautilus makes a little boat in which her eggs are laid. She stays with them until they hatch, and then she dies. A fish called a bitterling lays its eggs in the shell of a freshwater mussel. The eggs grow safely in the protection of the shell.

Most animals have no way of carrying things except in their mouths. Many mammals, such as cats, move their babies to safety in this way. Alligators and crocodiles are also caring mothers. They protect and carry their newly hatched young in their large jaws.

Some fish, called mouth breeders, hold their developing eggs or young in their mouths for long periods. Even after they are hatched, the babies stay close to their parents' heads so that they can rush back to the safety of the jaws. In some species, such as the cichlids, the female plays the nursemaid. In others,

▼ The female Nile crocodile shown here is carrying her newly hatched young from the nest to the river. Once in the water, the baby crocodiles have to find their own food, but their mother stays close to them and frightens away most creatures that might attack.

such as the South American sea catfishes, the males care for their families. They do not eat anything at all during the time that the young depend on them.

Some creatures have young that hang onto them. A newborn monkey or ape grasps the hair on its mother's underside. Later, it will ride on her back. Some babies seem to like being carried in this way. Opossums often look weighed down by several well-grown young.

FEMALE PANGOLIN WITH YOUNG ON BACK

Educating the Young

It is not likely that creatures such as scorpions, which protect their young by carrying them on their backs, teach their babies much. In other kinds of animals, particularly mammals and birds, the young ones learn a great deal from their elders. Usually they do this by observing and imitating.

For instance, young brown bears that have lost their parents never become such good fishers as those that have watched their mothers catch salmon.

Foxes educate their cubs by taking disabled prey to their den. The young ones learn how to make a kill under the watchful eyes of their parents.

FOX CUBS LEARNING HOW TO HUNT

▲ Pangolins usually have only one baby at a time. The mother carries the young one on her back, where it hangs on by curling its tail around hers. Sometimes baby animals seem unwilling to grow up and face the world on their own. A pangolin has been seen carrying a baby more than half her size. The baby clung to her so tightly that she was unable to dislodge it.

A SAFE HAVEN

Tree hornbills make the most secure nurseries for their chicks. The parents choose a suitable hole in a tree or a rock face. Then they plaster the entrance up with mud until the female can only just squeeze in. Once she is inside, the hole is made still smaller, until only a narrow slit remains open. Through this, the male hornbill passes food, nesting material, and snail shells, which provide calcium for the female.

When the baby hornbills hatch, they grow quickly so that they can reach the slit to be fed by their father. In spite of this growth, their feathers remain hidden beneath horny sheaths, so the chicks look almost like little porcupines. In some cases, the female leaves the chicks before they are full grown. They then use their droppings to remake the wall that keeps them safe from snakes and other predators.

▼ This red-billed hornbill is bringing fruit to feed his family, which is walled up in a hole in a tree. Most kinds of young hornbills remain in the nest for about a month and a half, so the male has to work very hard to provide food for them. He will not be able to rest and molt until his family has finally left the nest.

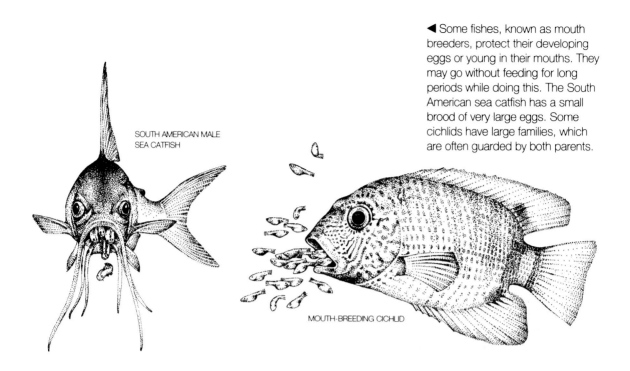

SOUTH AMERICAN MALE
SEA CATFISH

MOUTH-BREEDING CICHLID

◀ Some fishes, known as mouth breeders, protect their developing eggs or young in their mouths. They may go without feeding for long periods while doing this. The South American sea catfish has a small brood of very large eggs. Some cichlids have large families, which are often guarded by both parents.

Mound-Building Birds

Mound-building birds live in Australia and on various islands in the Pacific Ocean. They do not make nests and care for their young. Instead, their eggs are incubated by the heat of the ground. Some mound builders, such as the mallee fowl, make a compost heap of rotting vegetation and sand. The male uses his tongue as a thermometer to make sure that the temperature of the mound is right for the development of the eggs. He checks it every day and opens it up or adds more sand or vegetation. He works very hard for several months, for mallee fowls have a long breeding season. When the chicks hatch, they can fly almost immediately. They leave the area of the mound in which they developed and many never even see their parents.

MALE MALLEE FOWL
TENDING NEST MOUND

YOUNG MALLEE
FOWL EMERGING
FROM NEST MOUND

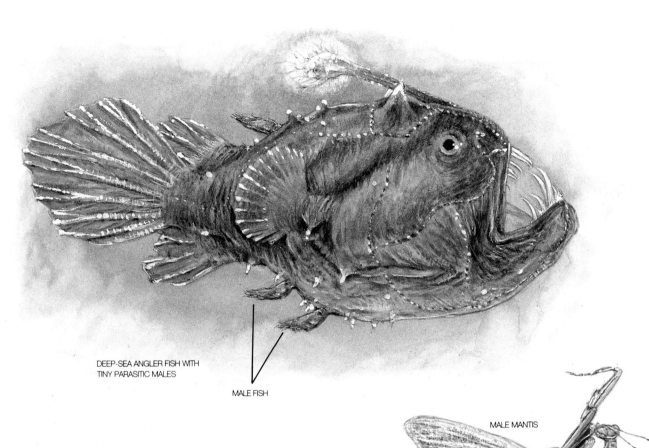

DEEP-SEA ANGLER FISH WITH
TINY PARASITIC MALES

MALE FISH

MALE MANTIS

FEMALE MANTIS

FEMALE MANTIS EATING
THE MALE AFTER MATING

STRANGE MATES

Some creatures have mates that look very different
from themselves. Many vary so in size and color that
scientists have given each of them a different name.
Usually there is a reason for these differences. Often the
males and females live apart for most the year and need
to be camouflaged in a different way. Differences in size
enable a pair of flesh eaters, such as birds of prey, to live
in a smaller area than would be possible if they were the
same size. Because they hunt different prey, they do not
compete with each other.

One of the greatest size differences can be seen
between the male and female paper nautilus. The
females are about a foot long, and the males are about
half an inch overall. Among deep-sea angler fish, the
males are also tiny. The females may grow to 3 feet in
length, but the males do not grow beyond 6 inches. Only
very young males have been found living alone. When a
male finds a female host, he becomes a parasite. He can
still breathe for himself, but she provides him with food,
and he can no longer survive alone.

▲ The size difference between the
male and female in some deep-sea
angler fish is greater than in other
vertebrates. Some females are ten
times larger than their parasitic mates.

Male and female praying
mantises are about the same size,
but their mating is one of the
strangest, for the female kills and
eats at least part of the male.

Changing Gender

Most creatures are born either male or female and remain the same sex throughout their lives. However, a few kinds of creatures are both male and female at the same time. Still others change from being one sex to the other.

For example, oysters start life as males. Later they change to females and still later they return to being males. Some fishes also change from being males to being females. Female jewfish, a kind of grouper, weigh over 660 pounds. The males are much smaller and change into females as they grow older. The opposite change takes place in a little coral reef fish called *Anthias*. Normally, groups of smaller females swim with a large male. If the male is caught or dies, the dominant female of the group takes over as leader and within two weeks has changed to a male.

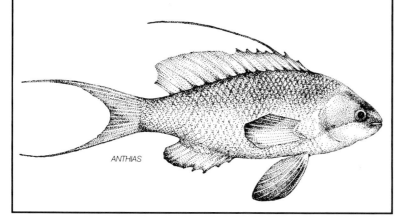

ANTHIAS

▼ Some creatures are both male and female at the same time. They are called **hermaphrodites**. Many land snails and slugs are hermaphrodites. They are male in the early part of the year and female later on. The eggs are fertilized as a result of an earlier mating. It is a good method of survival for animals that have many enemies, for every individual is able to add to the population.

EGG-LAYING MAMMALS

Mammals are furry, warm-blooded animals that normally give birth to babies that look much like their parents. There are two exceptions to this rule – the platypus, or duckbill, and two kinds of spiny anteaters. The platypus is found only in eastern Australia; anteaters live throughout Australia and in New Guinea. Other than their strange appearance, the thing that is odd about these mammals is that the females do not give birth in the normal way, but lay eggs, as birds and reptiles do.

Female platypuses lay their eggs in a nest made in a burrow by a stream. There are usually two eggs, about three fourths of an inch long. This is about the size of a sparrow's egg, though a platypus's weight may be more than a hundred times that of a sparrow. The eggs are kept warm against their mother's body for about two weeks. When they hatch, the babies stay in the burrow and are fed on milk for over four months.

A spiny anteater produces only one egg in a season. It is laid in a pouch on the female's belly. The egg hatches after ten days. The young animal remains in the pouch, where it feeds on its mother's milk for about three months.

▶ The nesting burrow of a platypus may be up to 65 feet long. It is made secure by a number of walls built across it so that any predator will think that the burrow is empty. Once the eggs have hatched, the female leaves the burrow to hunt for food, but she remakes the walls to protect her helpless young.

▼ This picture shows a baby spiny anteater in its mother's pouch. The female is lying on her back, and the opening of the pouch has been turned back a little so that the baby can be seen. It is still blind, helpless, and defenseless because its spines have not yet grown.

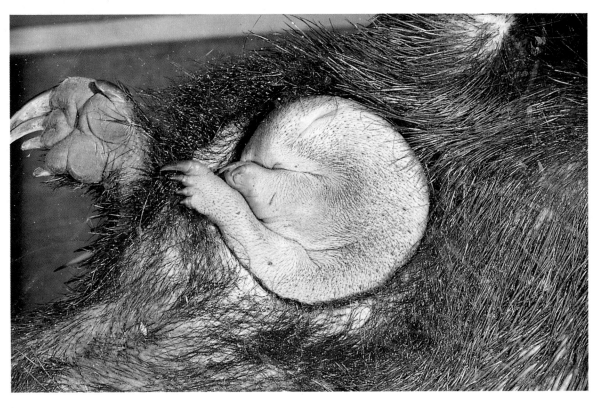

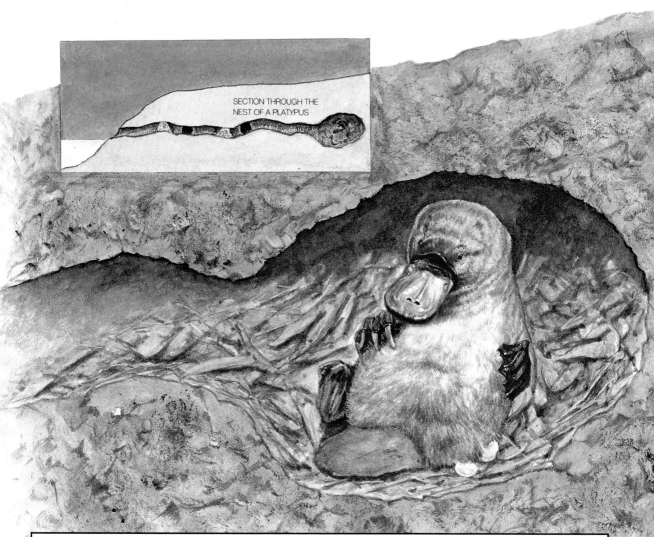

SECTION THROUGH THE
NEST OF A PLATYPUS

Milk for the Platypus

Like all other mammals, baby platypuses and spiny anteaters are fed on milk for the first part of their lives. In these species, the milk is produced differently from the way it is produced by other mammals. It flows from a number of **glands**, like sweat glands, on the underside of the female. Both the platypus and the anteaters have young with beaklike jaws. When they are hungry, they push at their mother's belly and lap up the milk. This must be a wasteful way of feeding, for some milk must be spilled. All other mammal babies suck milk directly into their mouths.

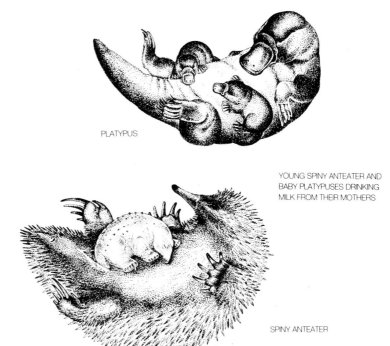

PLATYPUS

YOUNG SPINY ANTEATER AND
BABY PLATYPUSES DRINKING
MILK FROM THEIR MOTHERS

SPINY ANTEATER

SNAKE FLY LARVA

STAYING ALIVE

Animals may evade their enemies by living in strange places or having life-styles that protect them from attack. Some others escape being attacked because they surprise predators. A moment's hesitation by the hunter may be enough for the prey animal to get safely away.

HEADS OR TAILS?

In some animals, it is difficult to distinguish the head from the tail. This can fool predators. An attack to the head could be fatal, but it may do little damage to the tail. Some animals have large eye marks on their tail. This could prove very confusing to a hunter. If the real eyes are camouflaged, the deception is even better. Animals as different as fishes and butterflies use this trick. You can see how successful it is when you see a butterfly flying perfectly well with a piece of one of its hind wings missing. An eyespot may have been pecked away, but the butterfly has escaped with its life.

HAWK MOTH CATERPILLAR

THECLA BUTTERFLY

OWL BUTTERFLY

▲ Snake fly larvae can move backward almost as well as forward. If a predator digs into their tree bark home, they escape without turning around. It is difficult to decide which end is which of the *Thecla* butterfly, though it does not move backward very much. Eyespots can make a helpless animal look large and threatening.

34

In some butterflies the hind end of their wings is patterned and shaped to look like the front end of the body when the creature is at rest. Some butterflies can even move backward for short distances to make the illusion more complete.

FALSE-EYED FROG

▶ This butterfly fish has eye marks near its tail. This makes it difficult for a hunter to decide which end is the head. A fish may escape with an injured tail, but if its head is bitten, it is likely to be killed. As with many small animals, the defense is effective if it makes a predator hesitate for a moment – this may be long enough for it to escape.

Back-to-Front Burrowers

When danger threatens, animals that live in narrow spaces need to be able to move backward as fast as they move forward. The strange burrowing worm lizards can move backward as easily as forward and in some cases their tails are headlike in shape.

Some snakes, including the poisonous coral snake and the non-poisonous pipe snake, have brightly colored tails, sometimes with eye marks on them. These snakes pretend to attack, waving their tails in the air as if they were about to strike. This probably frightens away some attackers.

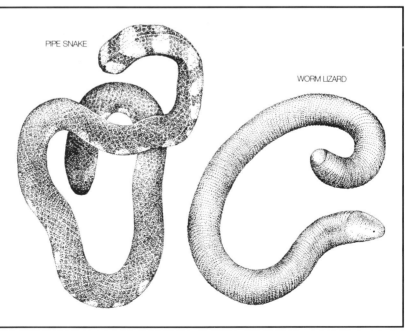

PIPE SNAKE

WORM LIZARD

BATS ROOSTING

UPSIDE-DOWN ANIMALS

Most animals live with their heads up. This means that their eyes and other sense organs are in a good position to detect sights and smells. Some creatures live an upside-down life, hanging from the branches and twigs of trees. This unusual posture is generally part of their camouflaged way of life. They rely on stillness to escape from being noticed. The largest upside-down animals are sloths. They hang, immobile, from strong, curved claws. The hairs of their long, shaggy coats are grooved and tiny plants grow in them. In its forest home, a sloth looks like any other bundle of vegetation hanging from a branch.

Bats spend their resting time hanging upside down. Their huge forelimbs and delicate wings, useful in flight, are not used now. At rest a bat's hind toes with large claws hang onto rough patches of bark or rock. The animal can relax in this position. Some bats have to maneuver to position themselves head-down against a wall. Horseshoe bats hang from the roofs of caves, somersault in flight and catch their foothold in one acrobatic movement. Then they fold their wings around their bodies.

▲ Bats spend most of their lives hanging upside down. They fly and feed for only a short time each day. When they are not fully active, bats tend to become sluggish. Their body temperature drops and their body functions slow down. This may enable them to hang head down without injury. Most mammals cannot hold their heads lower than the main part of their bodies without suffering.

36

Climbing the Wall

Geckos are little lizards. Most live in trees or among rocks. Some kinds have taken to living in houses, where they are usually welcome because they destroy flies and other insect pests. In the evening, house geckos come out from their hiding places and search for food. They often run up a wall and cross a ceiling upside down. They are able to do this because each toe has a series of large scales across it. Each scale has a number of fine hairs about $1/10$ millimeter long. There are about a million of these hairs on a gecko's feet. Each hair is branched and has flattened tips called spatulas. There may be 1,000 spatulas on a single hair. The pressure of these very tiny flattened hair tips holds the gecko securely as it runs across the ceiling.

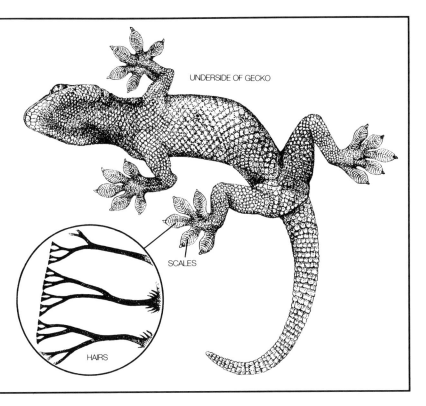

UNDERSIDE OF GECKO

SCALES

HAIRS

◀ Colugos, sometimes called flying lemurs, are the gliding champions of the world. Like the true mammalian fliers, the bats, they rest and move about the branches of trees upside down. They fold their huge flight membranes out of the way against their bodies. But as this picture shows, the wings make a convenient hammock for a baby.

CASSIOPEA

▲ This is a drawing of a beautiful tropical jellyfish called *Cassiopea*. Unlike most other jellyfish, it feeds on very tiny creatures, which are trapped in its frilly tentacles. To do this, it lies on its back on the seabed, creating small currents in the water to bring it food.

ESCAPING THE WEATHER

MONARCH BUTTERFLIES
HIBERNATING IN WINTER

Animals have many enemies apart from predators that want to eat them. The most important of these is the climate. If the weather is too hot, cold, dry, or wet, some animals will be likely to suffer. In spite of this, many creatures live where the weather may not be suitable for them all the time. They survive by being able to escape when conditions are not right.

Many creatures, from reindeer to hummingbirds and insects, migrate to escape unsuitable weather. They leave the area that no longer suits them and go to a place that does. Some just move up or down a mountainside. Others, for example bird migrants, travel many thousands of miles. Some hummingbirds could not survive their journey without a tail wind.

Other less mobile animals **hibernate** in cold weather. First they find a place that is likely to be free of frost. Once safely hidden, they drop into a deep, comalike sleep. They use little energy because their temperature drops, their heartbeat slows down, and their breathing rate decreases. This is easy for cold-blooded creatures like snakes and frogs because their body temperature is close to that of their surroundings. Mammals, which are warm-blooded, have to make great changes in the way their bodies work. Some of them have a **hibernation** sleep that lasts for about eight months of every year. They pack all their activity into the remaining third of the year. Perhaps because of this less stressful pace, they often live longer.

CONVERGENT LADYBUGS

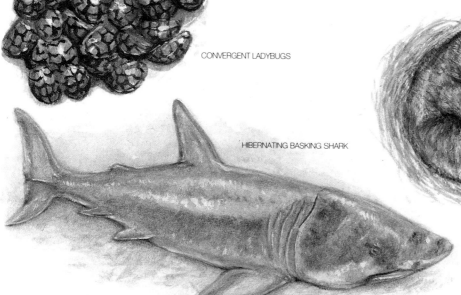

HIBERNATING BASKING SHARK

HIBERNATING WOODCHUCK

Sleeping Through the Heat
Some animals that live in hot parts of the world hide and sleep through the dry season. This sleep is very similar to hibernation, but it is called **estivation**. It starts when the weather gets very hot and food becomes scarce. Most animals prepare for estivation by eating a lot, for they will still use some energy even though they are inactive. Animals that estivate include some mammals, reptiles, insects, and even some kinds of fishes. Most find a cool, shady place well hidden from enemies. Some kinds of snails do not need to do this. They close the entrance to their shells with a hard paperlike substance and rest, often in blazing heat, until cool, moist weather returns.

▼ Many animals (see below) sleep through the winter. Cold-blooded creatures, such as reptiles and frogs, slip into hibernation easily. The same is true of insects. Some animals, such as the woodchuck, hibernate for nine months of each year, but badgers only sleep for part of the time.

▲ Many creatures breed in places that become too cold to survive in the winter. They migrate to escape the harsh weather. Most migrating birds, like these Brent geese, follow the sun from northern breeding grounds to warmer southern wintering places.

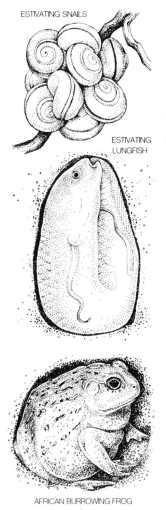

ESTIVATING SNAILS

ESTIVATING LUNGFISH

AFRICAN BURROWING FROG

NORTH AMERICAN BADGER IN WINTER SLEEP

MOTH PUPA WINTERING UNDERGROUND

MALE NARWHAL

STRANGE NATURE

The more we observe animals, the more strange things we find out about them. The reasons for some of these oddities are obvious. They help the creatures to survive in some way. Sometimes this is for a short period of its life. An example of this is a bird called the hoatzin. Hoatzins nest in low-growing branches by rivers in the tropical forests of South America. As with many birds, the chicks leave the nest before they can fly. They are able to scramble on the branches without falling into the water because they have clawed fingers on their wings. Because of this, hoatzins are able to use nest sites that would be too dangerous for the chicks of other birds.

▲ Female narwhals have no teeth, but the males have one long tooth which spirals like a long horn out of the front of the mouth. Nobody knows exactly how it is used. It is too fragile to be used as a weapon, but it may be used to stir up their diet of flatfish, from the seabed.

▼ When the heavy-bodied cockchafer beetle, or May bug, flies, it uses its hard wing cases to give it lift and beats its silvery hind wings. Since it flies at night, its large eyes and antennae warn it of obstructions and enemies.

LOOKING FOR ANSWERS

It is often impossible to say why an animal has a particular shape or way of life. The reason for this is that we still know very little about most kinds of animals. By watching them and seeing how they live, we may find answers. There are lots of common, easily seen creatures to find out about. Look at an earwig. Have you ever seen one fly? They do, sometimes. They have big wings, packed under tiny wing cases. So why don't they fly more often? By watching them you may find new ways of explaining strange nature.

HOATZIN CHICKS

HOATZIN ADULT

Useful Warts

It is easy to say that an animal is odd or ugly without thinking why that should be. The warthog is an example. We do not think the huge warts on its face are pretty, but there is a reason for them. In dry seasons, when most of the grass is eaten, some may remain under thorny bushes where other animals cannot go. The warthog can crawl beneath the thorns. If the thorns stick into the warts, and break off there, the warthog is not hurt. Later, in the rainy season, the warts swell with moisture and push the thorns out. The warthog's ugly warts protect it and help it to survive.

► Hoatzins nest in small branches overhanging streams. This is a safe place for the eggs, but once the young have hatched, they are in danger of falling into the water if they move from the nest. They rarely do so, however, because the chicks have long clawed fingers growing from their wings. These fingers help them to hold on.

WARTHOG

NATURAL TOOLS

The claws or other parts of the bodies of many creatures are adapted to get food from difficult places. The giraffe's long neck, the huge claws of an anteater, and the wirelike middle finger of an aye-aye are examples of these. Woodpeckers, which need to reach into the tunnels made by wood-boring grubs have a barbed or sticky tongue. The tongue is so long that when it is not in use it is wrapped around the bird's skull. Some animals have comblike claws or teeth that they use for grooming their fur. Some northern members of the grouse family grow special "snowshoe" feathers over their feet to protect them in wintertime. The varying lemming grows very large claws to help it dig in the snow.

AYE-AYE

AYE-AYE'S HAND
SHOWING LONG CLAW

CHAMELEON CATCHING AN INSECT

ANTEATER FEEDING

DIAGRAM TO SHOW
WOODPECKER WITH
TONGUE STORED

DIAGRAM TO SHOW
WOODPECKER WITH
TONGUE IN USE

▲ All these animals use parts of their bodies as tools. Aye-ayes use their middle fingers to pull insects from trees. Woodpeckers tap into an insect's tunnel with their beaks and then explore with their long tongues. Anteaters and chameleons use their long, sticky tongues to catch prey.

◄ The woodpecker finch from the Galapagos Islands has a fairly short, strong beak. It uses this to peck into the tunnels made by grubs in trees or large cactus plants. In other parts of the world, true woodpeckers pull the grubs out with their very long, sticky tongues. The woodpecker finch has a short tongue. It picks a long cactus thorn or a sharp twig to use as a tool to pull the grub out of its hole.

TOOL-USING ANIMALS

Sea otters live among giant seaweeds called kelps off the West Coast. They feed on creatures with hard shells that they gather from the bed of the sea. They have to dive to get their food, then they eat it above water. When a sea otter surfaces with a shell, it often brings a stone as well. It uses this as a hammer to break the shell.

Only chimpanzees, gorillas, and orangutans invent and make tools. Scientists had known that captive apes could solve problems, such as how to reach food outside their cages, by using sticks to pull it in. Recently, studies of chimpanzees in the wild have shown that they make and use simple tools. Unlike the tools used by creatures such as the sea otter, chimps change the detail of the implements they make, according to what needs to be done.

Living Tools

Some kinds of ants use their grubs, which produce silk, as living needles and threads. They hold the grubs and sew leaves together to make a suitable place for a nest in a tree. Other ants, which live in the deserts of Australia where there may not be much food for long periods, use some workers as living storage jars. When there is a good supply of nectar some ants known as "repletes" are fed on the surplus nectar. They are called "honey ants" or "honeypot ants" for their bodies swell until they look like little pots of honey. Unable to move, they hang by their legs until the food they contain is needed. Then it is removed and used throughout the nest.

HONEYPOT ANTS

STRANGEST OF ALL?

If you look at a garden, a park, a field, or a forest, you will find that the lives of the creatures that live there fit together in a complex pattern. But while you are looking, think about one other living thing – a species that is built like many four-legged animals, yet walks on only two legs. This can lead to all sorts of troubles, such as a bad back and aching feet, but it frees the forelimbs for holding and carrying things. It is a species that is clever but has so large a brain and head that birth is more difficult than it is for any other animal. It does many strange things, including destroying its environment and killing its own kind – something that hardly any other animal does. Yes, human beings are perhaps the strangest of all living things.

GLOSSARY

BACTERIA (singular: **BACTERIUM**) Some of the smallest and simplest of living things. The single cell that forms the body of a bacterium does not have a nucleus as animal cells do. Bacteria are found almost everywhere. They are very important because they break down the dead remains of plants and animals, returning them to the environment.

CAMOUFLAGE The way in which an object or an animal is colored and/or shaped, so that it is difficult to see.

CHRYSALIS The stage in the life of some insects, especially butterflies and moths, in which the changes from larva to adult take place. In most insects, this stage is called the pupa.

COLD-BLOODED Describes an animal whose body temperature changes with that of its surroundings. On a cold day it will have a low temperature; on a warm day its temperature may be far higher than that of a mammal. Because of this, it does not have a steady output of energy and can only be active when the weather is warm.

COLONY A group of the same kind of animals or plants living or growing together.

EMBRYO The earliest stage in an animal's development before it is born or hatches.

ENVIRONMENT The overall area in which an animal or a plant lives.

ESTIVATION A deep, comalike sleep in which some tropical animals pass the dry or very hot seasons. It is very similar to hibernation (see hibernation).

FUNGUS (plural: **FUNGI**) One of the major groups of living things. Fungi cannot make their own food, and as a rule they get it from plant or animal remains in the soil, or in some cases from living plants and animals. The most familiar fungi are mushrooms and toadstools, but there are many small forms, including molds and yeasts. Fungi are important because they break down dead animals and plants and return them to the soil.

GLANDS Small parts of an animal's body that make and release chemicals. Sweat glands produce a salty solution. Milk glands release a protein-rich liquid.

GRUB Another name for an insect larva (plural: larvae). See larvae.

HABITAT The natural home of a plant or an animal.

HERMAPHRODITE An animal, such as one of many snails, that is both male and female at the same time.

HIBERNATE To spend the winter in a completely inactive state called **HIBERNATION**. Hibernation is far more than sleep. The animal's heartbeat slows down, its body temperature drops, and its breathing rate decreases.

INSECTS Animals belonging to the large group called arthropods. The adult's body is divided into three parts. Insects have six legs and usually two pairs of wings.

INSULATE To separate something from its surroundings. We insulate ourselves from the cold with thick winter clothes. Other animals have fur, feathers, or a layer of fat.

LARVAE (singular: **LARVA**) Larvae are the young stages of some creatures. They are able to fend for themselves, but they look different and live and feed differently from their parents. When fully grown they change fairly rapidly to the adult form.

LICHENS A group of flowerless plants. Lichens are made of a fungus and an alga (a small green plant), living together in close association. They often encrust rocks or tree bark and hardly seem to be alive. Most grow very slowly and some are good indicators of clean air, for they cannot survive where there is pollution.

MAMMAL A warm-blooded air-breathing animal with a backbone, insulated in almost all cases with hair or fur. In the early stages of its life a mammal is fed on milk produced by its mother.

MIGRATE The movement, or **MIGRATION**, of a population of animals from one area to another. Usually there is a return movement later in the year.

MOSSES A group of non-flowering green plants, found in almost all parts of the world. Most are small and grow best in damp places, such as a moist woodland. They reproduce by spores that develop in capsules.

PARASITE A plant or an animal that lives in or on another (its host). The parasite takes food, protection, and support but gives nothing in return.

PREDATOR A hunter.

REPTILE An air-breathing, cold-blooded animal with a backbone. It has a hard, dry skin and in most cases the young hatch from eggs.

SCALE INSECTS Small insects that feed by sucking the juices of plants. Male scale insects look like small flies. Females are unlike all other adult insects, for they are wingless and often legless. Their soft bodies are protected by a hard covering, usually made of a waxy material.

SOCIAL INSECTS Insects that live in family groups, or colonies, where all the offspring are from one female, called the queen. The size of the colony varies. In termites and ants the colony is very large, whereas in some bees and wasps there are fewer than a 100 individuals.

TUNDRA A cold area of low-growing vegetation found in the far north of North America, Europe, and Asia. The subsoil is permanently frozen. The surface thaws during the short summer, to create waterlogged soil.

VIXEN A female fox.

WARM-BLOODED Describes an animal that has a constant high temperature, no matter how hot or cold its surroundings may be. Mammals and birds are warm-blooded animals. They have a steady output of energy, so they can be active during warm or cold weather, but they need a great deal of food to maintain a constant high body temperature.

INDEX

Illustrations are indicated in **bold**

A
African burrowing frog **39**
angler fish 30, **30**
anteater 42, **42**
Anthias 31, **31**
antifreeze fish 10, **11**
ants 18-19, **18**, **19**, 20, **22**, 43, **43**
aphids (greenfly) 19, **19**, 22, **22**, 23
aye-aye 42, **42**

B
badger **39**
barber fish 16, **16**
basilisk lizards 15, **15**
bats 36, **36**
bees 22
beetles 7, **7**, **12**, 18, 19, **19**, 21
bitterling 26
Brent geese 39, **39**
brown bears 27
butterflies **12**. 18, **18**
butterfly fish 35, **35**

C
Calliactis anemone **17**
camel 9
Cassiopea 37, **37**
cassowary **12**
chalk hill blue butterfly 18
chameleons 42, **42**
chimpanzees 43
cichlids 26, 29, **29**
clams 11, **11**
cleaner shrimps 16, **16**
cloak anemone 17, **17**
Clytostylus **7**
cockchafer (May bug) 40, **40**
colugos 37, **37**
coral snake 35
crab 11, **11**
crabeater seals 10, **10**
crocodiles 26, **26**

D
damselfish 17
Darwin's frog 24, **24**
decorator crabs 21, **21**
dodo **12**, 13

E
earwig 41
emu 8, **8**

F
false-eyed frog **35**
fisher spiders 14-15, **14**
foxes 24, 27, **27**
frogs 10, 24, **24-25**
fungus 20

G
gardener weevil 21, **21**
geckos 37, **37**
Gould's goanna **8**
grasshopper **12**

H
Halaeomysis 9, **9**
Hawaiian honeycreepers 13, **13**
hawk moth caterpillar **34**
hermit crabs 17, **17**
hip-pocket frog 24
hoatzin 40, 41, **41**
honey guides 17, **17**
honeypot ants 43, **43**
hornbills 28, **28**
humans 44, **44**

I
inland taipan **9**

J
jellyfish 37, **37**
jewfish 31

K
kiwi **12**
Komodo dragon 13, **13**
kowaris (desert mice) 8, **9**

L
ladybugs **38**
large blue butterfly 18, **18**
lily trotters 15, **15**
lizards 13, **13**, 15, **15**, 37, **37**
lungfish **39**

M
mallee fowl 29, **29**
moloch (thorny devil) **9**
Monarch butterflies **38**
monkeys 27
moon shell 26
musk oxen 9, **9**

N
naked mole rats 22-23, **23**
narwhals 40, **40**

O
opossums 27
orangutans 43
owl butterfly **34**

P
pangolins 27, **27**
paper nautilus 26, 30

parasitic fish 30
penguins 10
petrels 15, **15**
pipe fish 24, **25**
pipe snake 35, **35**
platypus 32, **33**
poison arrow frog **25**
polar bears 10
pond skaters 14, **14**
praying mantises 30, **30**

R
ratel (honey badger) 17, **17**
red-billed hornbill 28, **28**
rheas 25, **25**
rove beetle 19, **19**
    Lomechusa **19**
    Dinarda **19**

S
scale insects 20, **20**
sea anemones 17, **17**
sea horses 24, **24**
seals 10, **10**
Septobasidium 20, **20**
shark **38**
shrimp **6**
silvery blue butterfly 18
sloths 36
slugs 31
snails **31**, 39
snake fly larva 34, **34**
snakes 10
South American catfish 27, 29, **29**
spider crabs 21, **21**
spiny anteater 32, **32**, 33, **33**
sticklebacks 24, **24**

T
termites 17
Thecla butterfly **34**
toads 24
Trichaptus **7**

V
violin beetle **7**

W
water cricket **14**
water fleas 23, **23**
water measurer **14**
warthog 41, **41**
wasps 22
weevil 7, 21, **21**
whistling thorns 20, **21**
woodchuck (marmot) **38**
woodlouse **19**
woodpecker 42, **42**
woodpecker finch 43, **43**
worm lizard 35, **35**
worms 11, **11**

A TEMPLAR BOOK

Devised and produced by The Templar Company plc
Pippbrook Mill, London Road, Dorking, Surrey RH4 1JE
Copyright © 1992 by The Templar Company plc

PHOTOGRAPHIC CREDITS

t = top, b = bottom, l = left, r = right
Front cover Kim Taylor/Bruce Coleman Ltd
Back cover Kim Taylor/Bruce Coleman Ltd
Page 6 J. Pope; *page 9* H. Reinhard/Bruce Coleman Ltd;
page 10 I. Everson/Bruce Coleman Ltd; *page 13* J. & D. Bartlett/Bruce
Coleman Ltd; *page 15* K. Wothe/Bruce Coleman Ltd; *page 16* B. Wood/
Bruce Coleman Ltd; *page 19* B. Borrell/Frank Lane Picture Agency; *page 21*
M.P. Kahl/Bruce Coleman Ltd; *page 22* Kim Taylor/Bruce Coleman Ltd;
page 25 J. Burton/Bruce Coleman Ltd; *page 26* J. Visser/Bruce Coleman
Ltd; *page 28* G. Ziesler/Bruce Coleman Ltd; *page 31* A. Davies/Bruce
Coleman Ltd; *page 32* J. & D. Bartlett/Bruce Coleman Ltd; *page 35*
J. Burton/ Bruce Coleman Ltd; *page 37* P. Ward/Bruce Coleman Ltd;
page 39 R. Wilmhurst/Frank Lane Picture Agency; *page 40* Kim Taylor/
Bruce Coleman Ltd; *page 43* A. Root/Bruce Coleman Ltd.